Publisher's note:

Tintin, the intrepid reporter, first made his appearance January 10, 1929, in a serial newspaper strip with an adventure in the Soviet Union. From there, it was on to the Belgian Congo and then to America. Together with his dog, Snowy; an old seaman, Captain Haddock; an eccentric professor, Cuthbert Calculus; look-alike detectives, Thomson and Thompson; and others, Tintin roamed the world from one adventure to the next.

Tintin's dog, Snowy, a small white fox terrier, converses with Tintin, saves his life many times, and acts as his confidant, despite his weakness for whiskey and a tendency toward greediness. Captain Haddock, in some ways Snowy's counterpart, is a reformed lover of whiskey, with a tendency toward colorful language and a desire to be a gentleman-farmer. Cuthbert Calculus, a hard-of-hearing, sentimental, absent-minded professor, goes from small-time inventor to nuclear physicist. The detectives, Thomson and Thompson, stereotyped characters down to their old-fashioned bowler hats and outdated expressions, are always chasing Tintin. Their attempts at dressing in the costume of the place they are in make them stand out all the more.

The Adventures of Tintin appeared in newspapers and books all over the world. Georges Remi (1907–1983), better known as Hergé, based Tintin's adventures on his own interest in and knowledge of places around the world. The stories were often irreverent, frequently political and satirical, and always exciting and humorous.

Tintin's Travel Diaries is a new series, inspired by Hergé's characters and based on notebooks Tintin may have kept as he traveled. Each book in this series takes the reader to a different country, exploring its geography, and the customs, the culture, and the heritage of the people living there. Hergé's original cartooning is used, juxtaposed with photographs showing the country as it is today, to give a feeling of fun as well as education.

If Hergé's cartoons seem somewhat out of place in today's society, think of the time in which they were drawn. The cartoons reflect the thinking of the day, and set next to modern photographs, we learn something about ourselves and society, as well as about the countries Tintin explores. We can see how attitudes have changed over the course of half a century.

Hergé, himself, would change his stories and drawings periodically to reflect the changes in society and the comments his work would receive. For example, when it was originally written in 1930, *Tintin in the Congo*, on which *Tintin's Travel Diaries: Africa* is based, was slanted toward Belgium as the fatherland. When Hergé prepared a color version in 1946, he did away with this slant. Were Hergé alive today, he would probably change many other stereotypes that appear in his work.

From the Congo, Tintin went on to America. This was in 1931. Al Capone was notorious, and the idea of cowboys and Indians, prohibition, the wild west, as well as factories, all held a place of fascination. *Cigars of the Pharaoh* (1934) introduced Hergé's fans to the mysteries of Egypt and India. A trip to China came with *The Blue Lotus* in 1936, the first story Hergé thoroughly researched. After that, everything was researched, including revisions of previous stories. *The Land of Black Gold*, for example, an adventure in the Middle East, was written in 1939, and revised in 1949 and again in 1969.

Although *The Broken Ear* introduced readers to the Amazon region in 1935, the story was pure fantasy, complete with imaginary countries. In 1974 the adventure continued with *Tintin and the Picaros*, Hergé's last story. When *The Seven Crystal Balls*, which was serialized from 1943 to 1944, was continued in 1946, Hergé began to give the reader factual information about pre-Columbian civilization with marginal notes titled "Who were the Incas?" *Tintin in the Land of the Soviets* was Tintin's first adventure, in 1929, and the only one not to be redone in color.

Tintin's Travel Diaries are fun to read, fun to look at, and provide educational, enjoyable trips around the world. Perhaps, like Tintin, you, too, will be inspired to seek out new adventures!

The publisher particularly wishes to thank Mrs. Christine Ockrent and television channel Antenne 2 for their kind permission to use the title *Travel Diaries*.

THE AMAZON
AND THE AMERICAS

TINTIN'S TRAVEL DIARIES

A collection conceived and produced by Martine Noblet.

Les films du sable thank the following **Connaissance du monde** photographers for their participation in this work:

Jacques Cornet, Gerard Civet, Luc Giard,
Anne-Sophie Tiberghien,
Claude Jannel, and Michel Aubert

The authors thank Christiane Erard and
Daniel De Bruycker for their collaboration.

All inquiries should be addressed to:
Barron's Educational Series, Inc.
250 Wireless Boulevard
Hauppauge, New York 11788

Library of Congress Catalog Card No. 94-36957

International Standard Book No. 0-8120-6489-5 (hard cover)
International Standard Book No. 0-8120-9160-4 (paperback)

Library of Congress Cataloging-in-Publication Data

Noblet, Martine.
   The Amazon and the Americas / text by Martine Noblet and
Chantal Deltenre ; translation by Maureen Walker.
      p.   cm. — (Tintin's travel diaries)
   Includes bibliographical references (p.   ) and index.
   ISBN 0-8120-6489-5. — ISBN 0-8120-9160-4 (pbk.)
   1. Amazon River Region—Description and travel—Juvenile
literature.   2. Latin America—Description and travel—Juvenile
literature.   [1. Amazon River Region.   2. Latin America.   3. Cartoons
and comics.]   I. Deltenre, Chantal.   II. Title.   III. Series.
F2546.N7   1995
981'.1—dc20
                                                              94-36957
                                                                 CIP
                                                                 AC

j 918.11

Printed in Hong Kong
5678   9927   987654321

THE AMAZON
AND THE AMERICAS

Text by Martine Noblet and Chantal Deltenre
Translation by Maureen Walker

BARRON'S

In rereading Tintin's adventures, I was surprised to see that, along with my eight brothers and sisters, I have very often run into Tintin, preceded him, or followed him. The Mahuziers in Africa, Australia, North America, Russia, Nepal, Ladakh, Zanskar, Tibet…or even Siberia, Central Asia, Japan, and so on, — 22 grand adventures…I was going to say, 22 Tintin books. The twenty-third would have made it possible for us to share one of the best works ever produced by the World Tour family: the Mahuziers on the Amazon river, six long trips looking for treasure that Tintin and the Mahuziers have always sought: knowledge of the world, knowledge of other people, and friendship among people.

Tintin, honorary member of the Mahuzier Tribe: we would be proud, since we are making our way along the same road. Tintin, Nobel Peace Prize winner—why not?

YVES MAHUZIER

While paddling up the Amazon River in a dugout canoe, I ventured upon extraordinary things that no other stream on earth can provide. As an avid reader of Tintin in my youth, I am sure he would have loved to have joined me in that adventure.

In the middle of the Amazon, floating islands drift gently down-stream—almost impossible to believe, Professor Calculus would say. But indeed, such islands exist. They are in fact large chunks of forests with trees, roots, grass mats, and soil, broken loose from sharp bends of the river by the flooding waters higher upstream and sent on their way down in the main current.

Tintin would have seen with delight that some of these islands were big enough to carry Indian huts with cheering families, and he would have loved to have shared this adventure. Snowy would have been eager to jump on board these islands but afraid to swim in the river among the piranhas.

But floating islands last only for a short time. The fate of many is to end up floating down to the immense mouth of the Amazon, becoming carefully watched navigational hazards before eventually sinking to the depths of the ocean.

Tintin would have remembered with nostalgia the story of the floating islands with their gentle Indians; Snowy would have been happy not to have had wet feet among the piranhas; Calculus would eventually have understood the real story; and the detectives Thomson and Thompson would remain utterly frustrated because there was no real mystery to investigate—they would have been fooled by a marvelous trick of nature.

ALBERT V. CAROZZI

CONTENTS

The words in **boldface** are found in the glossary on page 70.

HOW DID THE AMAZON RIVER GET ITS NAME?

A misunderstanding by an explorer, lost on the giant river around 1540, caused it to become known in Europe as the river "of the Amazons." He believed he had been fighting "warrior women" there.

Attacked by the long-haired Yagua warriors, **Francisco de Orellana**, the lieutenant of the conquistador Pizarro, thought they were women, cousins of the legendary Amazons of antiquity. However, the river's local name, O-rio-mar, the sea-river, seems much more appropriate to its huge size.

With its 4,000-mile (6,500 km) length and thousands of tributaries, the **Amazon** is indeed the most powerful of all the earth's rivers. Through its 90-mile (140 km) wide mouth, almost 80 billion gallons (302.83 billion l) of fresh water an hour (or 50 times the output of the Nile, and 12 times the output of the Mississippi) flow into the Atlantic Ocean, pushing the salt water up to 63 miles (101.4 km) out to sea!

Its basin holds all the records, too. From the Andes to the Atlantic, three times the total area of Texas, Florida, Georgia, Alabama, Indiana, Arizona, Utah, Rhode Island, and Oregon, the Amazon area is a huge bowl with an almost flat bottom where the river and its tributaries wind back and forth in endless meanders, usually extending over several miles wide. During floods, the waters submerging the forest often cover 25 miles (40.2 km) or more from side to side, washing away portions of the banks, which become floating islands. The Amazon leaves behind it marshy areas, sometimes as big as four-fifths the size of Texas.

Top: The winding Amazon River
Bottom: Climbing the rapids in the Amazon River

WHAT IS THE "IGAPO"?

A thick, marshy forest in the Amazon region, the igapo is the kingdom of tortoises, crocodiles, fish, crabs, and otters.

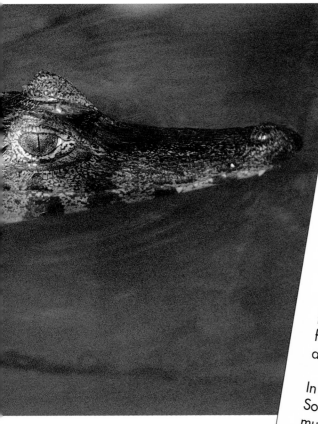

The Amazonian **selva**, a Portuguese word, is a humid forest watered constantly by equatorial rains and often soaked by flooded rivers as well. Consequently, the soil is swampy. Though the big trees do well there, with their tops in the sun and their roots in the water, animals have to make a choice: they must either be good swimmers or live their lives in the treetops.

Thus the forest shelters two clearly differentiated levels. At the top, perched 130 feet (40 m) up, is a sunny, luxuriant world whose sweet-smelling flowers and fat berries feed a whole population of birds, acrobat-monkeys, and butterflies. Down below, even the ground, spongy and water-logged, is plunged into perpetual dusk, because the dense foliage lets in barely 1 percent of the daylight. Debris falling from the trees rots among the roots, mosses, and ferns, or is gobbled up by crustaceans, fish, reptiles, frogs, and all sorts of mammals.

In this amphibious world, there are all kinds of creatures: Some fish evolved lungs to breathe at the surface of the muddy water; some even climb trees, like one species of catfish; and some frogs choose to live high up….

Top: An alligator
Left: The swamps in the "selva"
Right: A butterfly in the Amazon rain forest

WHAT IS THE "GREEN HELL"?

Tangled up in the vegetation, overcome by the humid heat and insects, and weakened by fever, the few Europeans who ventured into the Amazon region often met their death there...

There is no other selva like this one. Never cleared by human beings, it is virgin, so-called primary, forest: There is no single dominant plant life, but all grow closely packed, even one on another, like lianas and orchids. Crowding together to catch the slightest ray of light, the big trees compete in height: up to 130 feet (40 m) in the humid zone, and twice that wherever the ground is firmer.

It is a titanic world, with trees unknown elsewhere such as the mahogany tree, the Brazilian rosewood tree, the famous hevea, or rubber tree that the Indians call **caoutchouc** (its sap provides us with rubber), and the brazilwood tree—whose wood, the color of glowing coals, gave its name to Brazil. Close to 100,000 other species make up the wealth of the botanical paradise, from strychnos (whose toxic resin is used to produce curare) to the Victoria water lily, with its gigantic tray-shaped leaves.

In the depths of the forest, even today, science is still discovering unknown plants, from which some of tomorrow's medicines will be derived. Animals also benefit from the botanical diversity. Some that are no longer found anywhere else on earth, like the **tapir**, have found in the Amazon region an "ecological niche" that suits them.

Top: An Indian canoe
Bottom: Victoria regia (water lilies)

CAN YOU SWIM IN THE AMAZON?

Despite the terrible reputation of certain fish, bathing in the Amazon does not amount to suicide: The piranhas do not gobble up everything that moves!

Piranhas, those terrors of the Amazon, are primarily river carrion-eaters who clear away animals drowned in the floods, and diseased or wounded animals. The victims are dismembered within a few minutes by the strong jaws and sharp teeth of these little carnivorous fish, which, attracted by blood, flock to join in the feast. If piranhas were as voracious as is claimed, there would be nothing left in the river except for them. In fact, piranhas attack humans only during their mating season. But, the Amazon region is home to thousands of aquatic species, including a few residents that are equally disquieting...

Many river inhabitants are giants, from the electric eel (whose electrical discharges can stun an ox) to the famous anaconda, a water python that can grow up to 32 feet (9.75 m) long. We must not forget the matamata tortoise or the pirarucú, the very long pike whose 297 pounds (134.7 kg) of flesh feed many riverbank dwellers. **Caymans** infest certain rivers, too, as well as bold **leeches** that are so hard to get rid of.

Equally amazing are the pink dolphin, the giant otter, and the placid manatee that browses on the algae along the banks.

Left: An anaconda snake
Right: A piranha

WHICH ANIMAL HAS THE LONGEST TONGUE?

The tamandua, or Amazonian great anteater, has a tongue as long as it is fine: nearly 2 feet (60 cm), so it can reach ants and termites in the depths of their nests.

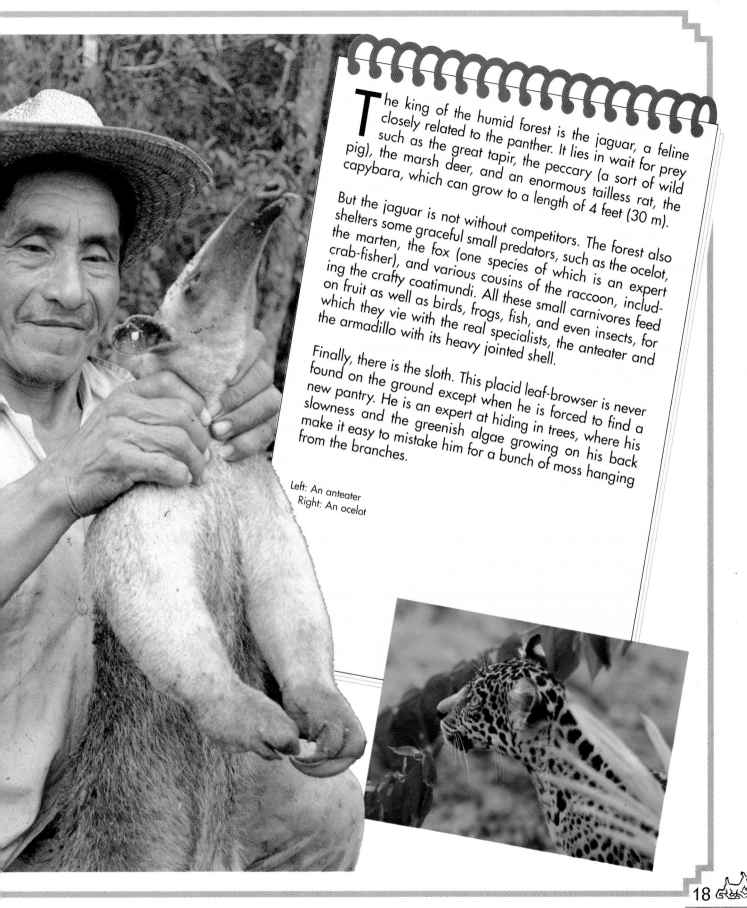

The king of the humid forest is the jaguar, a feline closely related to the panther. It lies in wait for prey such as the great tapir, the peccary (a sort of wild pig), the marsh deer, and an enormous tailless rat, the capybara, which can grow to a length of 4 feet (30 m).

But the jaguar is not without competitors. The forest also shelters some graceful small predators, such as the ocelot, the marten, the fox (one species of which is an expert crab-fisher), and various cousins of the raccoon, including the crafty coatimundi. All these small carnivores feed on fruit as well as birds, frogs, fish, and even insects, for which they vie with the real specialists, the anteater and the armadillo with its heavy jointed shell.

Finally, there is the sloth. This placid leaf-browser is never found on the ground except when he is forced to find a new pantry. He is an expert at hiding in trees, where his slowness and the greenish algae growing on his back make it easy to mistake him for a bunch of moss hanging from the branches.

Left: An anteater
Right: An ocelot

6   IS THE VIRGIN FOREST SILENT?

At ground level, the dark forest is a world of silence compared to the treetops where the din of parrots, toucans, and howler monkeys resounds.

The treetop world, brightly colored under the dazzling sun, is called the canopy. Most of its inhabitants never see the ground.

Snakes, cats, carnivorous bats, spiders, crested eagles, and other predators disguise themselves as best they can, stalking their prey among the foliage. Those whom nature has not provided with wings, like the monkeys, some species of squirrels, and frogs, owe their survival to their talents as acrobats or gliders. Others hardly bother to hide, trusting to the alarm signals of their brothers on sentinel duty, like the howler monkeys do...

Those who have wings readily take on all the colors of the rainbow, like the sparkling hummingbirds and the **toucans** with their huge, gaudy beaks. But the stars are obviously the parrots, whose many species, from the big blue and yellow macaws to the delicate parakeets, bring to the multicolored spectacle the strident sounds of a constant cacophony.

Top: A toucan
Bottom: The Isle of Monkeys on Leticia in Colombia

WHERE DOES RUBBER COME FROM?

Plant products have always been the Amazon region's prime wealth: exploitation of the colored brazilwood, and especially rubber, derived from the sap of the hevea tree.

Botanists had long been aware of the properties of latex but found no other uses for it beyond those already discovered by the Indians: waterproofing footwear and clothing, and making balls to play with. It was the **inflatable tire**, that indispensable accessory of the automobile, invented in 1888, that made the Amazon region's fortune, and specifically the fortunes of the cities of Iquitos in Peru and Manaus in Brazil.

Here, thousands of miles from urban civilization, in the heart of the virgin forest crisscrossed by tappers known as "seringueiros," the renowned **Fitzcarraldo** and other "rubber barons" lived a life of staggering opulence for a while, importing from Europe and paying fortunes for them, their wives' clothes, marble for their homes, and even singers for the Manaus opera house, brought all the way there by deep-sea freighters. The vessels then went back down the river loaded with precious latex.

About 1876, Sir Robert Wickham, an English agent, managed to smuggle out a few hevea seeds, which he successfully replanted in Ceylon and the Malay Peninsula: This seriously affected South America's industry. Later, the appearance of synthetic rubber, derived from petroleum, put an end to the "soft gold" fever and the ostentatious lifestyle of its magnates. Perhaps, one day, the as-yet little-known resources of the flora of the jungle, rich in medicinal plants, will bring a new golden age to the region.

Left: A Yanomami Indian climbs a scaffold to gather nuts from a tree
Right: A tree in the Amazon rain forest

WHY IS THE AMAZON REGION CALLED THE "LUNG OF THE WORLD"?

The equatorial forest plays an essential part in the renewal of our planet's oxygen. Nearly one-third of this forest worldwide is located in the Amazon region.

The Amazonian forest is a powerful regenerator of the world's atmosphere, and it is vital that this huge "green zone" be preserved. Yet, every day in Brazil, the forest loses over 31 square miles (50 sq. km) from **deforestation**—mainly as a result of mining operations. Also a factor is the clearing of countless little tracts of land on which peasants fleeing overpopulated areas come to settle.

Now the tropical forest, rich and luxuriant in appearance, actually grows on soil that is poor and fragile. The thin layer of fertile topsoil, when exposed to the open air, is quickly washed away by the rains or blown away by the wind. The deforested areas become deserts, to the despair of colonists who wanted to make a living there. All that is left for them, once the land has been ruined, is the depressing prospect of going back to the shantytowns encircling the big cities, to look for a less dramatic situation.

Behind them, the forest will not grow back. And the Indians, the only ones capable of living in harmony with it, will not come back again either.

The Transamazonian Highway

WHO ARE THE INDIANS OF THE AMAZON REGION?

Traveling over the frozen Bering Strait, the first Indians moved steadily from North America to South America. Some settled in the Amazon region about 10,000 years ago.

Guaranis, Tupis, **Yanomamis**...the forest Indians comprise several peoples and numerous tribes. Though they all have in common a way of life suited to the natural setting, each has its own language, religion, traditions, and social system.

The Indians live in groups scattered over vast areas and, with few exceptions, in communities not exceeding 200 people. They live in perfect harmony with the forest, that protective, magical universe where everything depends on the supernatural. To come close to "the beyond," and to stay constantly in touch with the higher spirits is therefore a vital necessity. This kind of encounter takes place under the guidance of a **shaman**, with the use of drugs.

But the folly of "civilized" men now sends up in smoke, every years, millions of acres of Amazonian forest that for the Indians has been a magical refuge. In order to preserve a habitat for the Indians, in 1991 the Brazilian government issued decrees reserving land for their exclusive use.

Top: Yanomami children in the upper Orinoco Delta
Bottom: Young Xingu Indian boy in Brazil

WHO INVENTED THE BLOWPIPE?

The Indians created this accurate silent weapon made of a long hollow tube. A puff of breath propels a dart, the tip of which is sometimes coated with a rapidly acting poison: curare.

Not all Indians hunt with blowpipes: Depending on the game, they use spears, bows, or traps, while certain tribes prefer fishing with bows, harpoons, or nets. The Indians also enjoy the results of gathering; however, these are just extras compared to **manioc**, which they grow in forest clearings. The open land, cleared by burning the original vegetation, will be reclaimed by the forest as soon as the soil begins to be depleted.

In this stifling climate, where it is only possible to work early in the morning and late in the evening, Indian life leaves a lot of time for leisure and ceremonies, as well as for preparing for them: making personal ornaments and designing body painting first, then dances, songs, and games. Magic and the dreams brought on by tobacco or traditional drugs maintain continuous contact with rites and festivals. All these activities perpetuate the memory and the traditions of the Indian tribes. They celebrate the close alliance between men, the natural world around them, and the magical presence of spirits.

Top: Hunting with a blowpipe
Bottom: Coreguaje village chief, Penilla River, Amazon Basin, Colombia

DO THE JIVAROS STILL SHRINK HEADS?

Missionaries and governments have forbidden this Indian tribe living on the borders of the Amazon region to practice its essential rite. But what goes on far away from society, in the depths of the Amazonian forest?

From the time Columbus landed in the New World, missionaries (especially the **Jesuits**) tried to convert and "re-educate" the Indians, often risking their lives in the process. By concentrating these nomads in villages constructed around the missions, forcing them to wear European clothing, and forbidding polygamy and many other customs (including their language, which the missionaries attempted to simplify), the missionaries tried to bring to these so-called "savages" the salvation of their souls and a more "humane" way of life.

What the missionaries accomplished was to deprive these populations of all their reasons for living: Even more than the diseases imported from Europe, the colonists' rifles, or working on the plantations, despair weakened and decimated the Indians.

In the sixteenth century, 3 million Indians lived in Brazil. Today there are barely 150,000 left. FUNAI (the National Foundation for Indians) is trying to protect them from the pressure of gold prospectors and big lumber companies. A press campaign led by the singer Sting and the **cacique** Raoni certainly brought public awareness to the genocide of the Yanomamis, but for many other tribes, it is already too late…

Top: Xingu Indian, Brazil
Bottom left: Shrunken head (Belem Museum)
Bottom right: Loss of traditions in the Indian culture

WHAT ARE THE GREAT INDIAN CIVILIZATIONS?

From the Andes to Mexico, many Indian peoples have left impressive traces showing a high level of culture.

Like the Inca of Peru, the peoples of Mexico were ambitious builders. The famous **Aztec** were among a number of refined cultures: those of the **Toltec**, the **Olmec**, and the learned **Maya**. Archaeologists have been unearthing their pyramids, abandoned over five hundred years ago, and other monuments to their civilizations.

Many other peoples, however, lived without building stone palaces. In their case, the wealth of craftsmanship in pottery, wickerwork, and weaving, the expressiveness of their language, the charm of their legends, or the complexity of their religion, attest to past splendor.

It is a wonderful fact that more than one people found the inner strength to maintain part of their heritage up to the present, despite slavery that devalued old customs, imposed compulsory learning of Spanish or Portuguese, and forced the adoption of Christianity. Traditional arts and local languages have thus persisted secretly in families and villages.

Top: The Maya ruins in Palenque
Bottom: Palenque: Mayan temple ruins

32

33

DOES THE AMAZONIAN FOREST COVER THE WHOLE OF BRAZIL?

Though the Amazonian forest is immense, Brazil, the largest country in South America, is even more immense. It is 3,286,502 square miles (8,511,999 sq. km), larger than the 48 contiguous U.S. states. Fertile regions, plateaus covered with grasslands, and desert zones are found there.

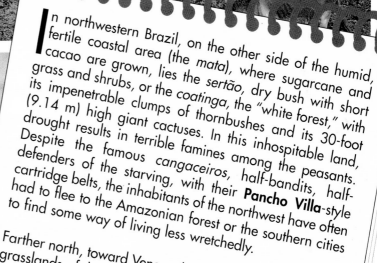

In northwestern Brazil, on the other side of the humid, fertile coastal area (the *mata*), where sugarcane and cacao are grown, lies the *sertão*, dry bush with short grass and shrubs, or the *coatinga*, the "white forest," with its impenetrable clumps of thornbushes and its 30-foot (9.14 m) high giant cactuses. In this inhospitable land, drought results in terrible famines among the peasants. Despite the famous *cangaceiros*, half-bandits, half-defenders of the starving, with their **Pancho Villa**-style cartridge belts, the inhabitants of the northwest have often had to flee to the Amazonian forest or the southern cities to find some way of living less wretchedly.

Farther north, toward Venezuela, are the *llanos*, the great grasslands of the Orinoco plain that shelter vast herds of cattle, like the plateaus of the Mato Grosso and the monotonous marshy *campos* of the Gran Chaco, between Bolivia and Paraguay.

Finally there is the endless Argentinian *pampa* and the world of the *gauchos*, the cowboys of Latin America who drive the cattle over vast expanses of land from one hacienda to another. But by this time, it's not Brazil anymore...

Top: The sertão, Brazil
Bottom: Vaqueros (Brazilian cowboys)

WHAT IS SLASH-AND-BURN FARMING?

Slash-and-burn farming consists of clearing part of the forest by burning the vegetation. The ashes enrich the inhospitable soil for a few years. All that remains to be done is to sow...

This type of farming was long the way the nomadic Indians made their living, moving on as soon as the soil began to be exhausted and clearing a new patch farther away.

But slash-and-burn farming brought about the ruination of the colonists who followed the Indians. Forced to remain on the bit of land allocated to them by the government, the poor Brazilian farmers, fleeing the overcrowded regions of the northeast, watched their new property grow sterile. Many of them turned to other hard, poorly paid, and often dangerous jobs: They became latex harvesters, woodcutters, or prospectors for gold and precious stones, constantly pushing the Indians farther back into the forest. Most, however, became discouraged in the end and, as a last resort, fell back to the industrial suburbs, where they frequently encountered the same fate of insecurity and poverty.

In other regions, country life is no easier, except for the fortunate owner of a huge plantation or a **fazenda**. The fate of the *vaqueiros* (cowherds), like that of the agricultural workers who harvest sugarcane, coffee, or bananas, is thus subject to the whims of an all-powerful employer, on lands often devoted to a single type of crop.

Left: A farmer in Brazil
Right: Burning the fields

IS GOLD FOUND IN BRAZIL?

The Brazilian state operates some rich gold mines, alongside 875,000 "garimpeiros," self-employed gold prospectors, who dig into the earth in conditions that are often atrocious.

After the conquest of the New World, while the Spanish were dreaming of El Dorado, the Portuguese, busy with trade in spices from the Indian peninsula, and in exotic woods and ivory from Africa, showed no interest in the new Brazilian lands except to set up gigantic sugarcane plantations. The result, from the point of view of the indigenous populations, was hardly preferable: Already familiar with the slave trade in Africa, the Portuguese sent **bandeirantes**, soldiers of fortune, to capture Indians in the hinterland, in order to supply the plantations with manpower.

During one of these manhunts, the colonists discovered the rich gold, silver, and diamond fields in the **Minas Gerais** region. The gold rush started immediately and lasted for over a century. The city of Ouro Prêto still shows evidence of this time in its sumptuous Baroque-style churches and its dream-homes, built by the luckier prospectors. Today Brazil is the world's sixth-ranked gold-producing country. A veritable belt of the precious ore is said to extend from the state of Rondônia, in the southwestern Amazon region, all the way to the Atlantic coast. So mining continues, but often at the expense of the Indians who are denied their country's wealth.

Left: The garimpeiros (gold miners) of the Serra Pelada
Right: The garimpeiros, hard at work

WHY IS SOUTH AMERICA CALLED "LATIN AMERICA"?

Colonized by the Spanish and the Portuguese, the entire southern half of the New World adopted the languages of its overseas conquerors, who were of Latin culture.

Impelled by their thirst for gold, the Spanish conquistadores launched their conquest of Mexico from bases set up in the Antilles by Christopher Columbus. Then, following the Pacific coastline, they turned southward to conquer the Incan Empire, and northward to California. The Portuguese, also great explorers, landed on South America's Atlantic coast, easily accessible from their colonies in Africa and the Azores.

Thus colonized on its west and east sides at the same time, South America was soon divided up, in the Treaty of Tordesillas in 1494, between the Portuguese who settled in what was later to become Brazil, and the Spanish who occupied the rest of the continent. Both made their languages compulsory.

After the independence of the various countries that now constitute Latin America, emigrants of every origin came to seek their refuge or fortune, joining the black slaves long present already. Italians, Germans, and even Japanese make up important communities in various countries. But depending on the country involved, the official language has continued to be that of the first conquerors.

The Spanish explorer Orellana, who discovered the Amazon

IS SOUTH AMERICA ALWAYS INVOLVED IN REVOLUTIONS?

Though some countries now have stable democratic governments, military coups d'état and guerrillas have not completely vanished.

A
LAS DOPICOS

A MORT ALCAZAR

A MORT ALCAZAR

M any Latin American countries owe their beginnings to a revolution. Most have had, and many still do have, a very turbulent political history, due in part to the huge contrast between the rich and powerful elite, often descendants of the first colonists, and the rest of the population: Indians, the children of slaves and racially mixed marriages, and immigrants. The social tension was so acute that the disadvantaged regularly revolted. The privileged then resorted to force to preserve their status.

Thus power fell into the hands of dictators who, having no need of electors, could adopt extreme measures, or of **juntas** of officers who ran their country like a barracks. Even reformers inspired by an ideal of progress, like Juan **Perón** in Argentina, sometimes became despots in order to pursue their reforms unhindered. They ended up plunging their countries into civil war.

Fear of political change and instability has also induced some Latin American leaders to align their countries with more powerful nations. Thus, for a long time many Latin American countries were influenced by regional powers such as the United States.

Top: Military parade on "Sea Day" in La Paz
Bottom: Bolivian soldiers

WHAT RELIGION DO LATIN AMERICANS PRACTICE?

Except for a few Indian villages that are cut off from the rest of the world, Christianity is the dominant faith of the entire continent. But it is practiced in 1001 different ways...

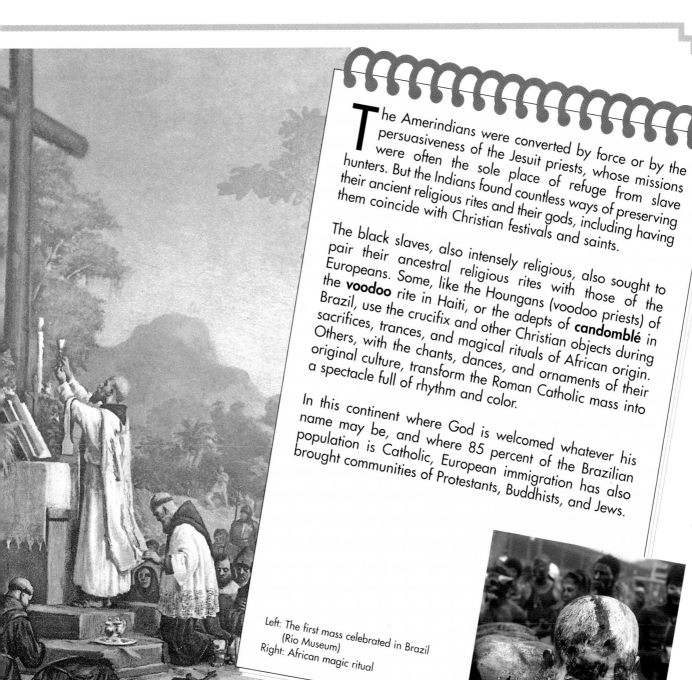

The Amerindians were converted by force or by the persuasiveness of the Jesuit priests, whose missions were often the sole place of refuge from slave hunters. But the Indians found countless ways of preserving their ancient religious rites and their gods, including having them coincide with Christian festivals and saints.

The black slaves, also intensely religious, also sought to pair their ancestral religious rites with those of the Europeans. Some, like the Houngans (voodoo priests) of the **voodoo** rite in Haiti, or the adepts of **candomblé** in Brazil, use the crucifix and other Christian objects during sacrifices, trances, and magical rituals of African origin. Others, with the chants, dances, and ornaments of their original culture, transform the Roman Catholic mass into a spectacle full of rhythm and color.

In this continent where God is welcomed whatever his name may be, and where 85 percent of the Brazilian population is Catholic, European immigration has also brought communities of Protestants, Buddhists, and Jews.

Left: The first mass celebrated in Brazil
(Rio Museum)
Right: African magic ritual

IS THERE RACISM IN BRAZIL?

Melancholy like a Portuguese, enjoying life like an African, dress-conscious like an Indian: it is said that the character of the Brazilian is a harmonious blend of his various origins.

Mixing together the most diverse races—or racial blending—is nothing new in Brazil. The first Portuguese colonists often took black or native women as their companions. The children of these inter-racial unions, became servants, employees, or self-employed small farmers, and took their place between the rich white landowner minority and the black slave masses, two-thirds of the population around 1880. The end of slavery, which did not occur until 1888, and the arrival of millions of European and Japanese immigrants, who were far less well off than the descendants of the first colonists, only partially modified the differences of rank between the three traditional components of Brazilian society.

Even though a few sons of slaves have been successful in show business and soccer, and though, conversely, some white peasants in the Northeast have ended up poverty-stricken in the **favelas**, the poverty is so pervasive and the educational opportunities few for people of non-European descent, that inequalities in social conditions are perpetuated from generation to generation.

Thus, although there is great tolerance among the races themselves, the financial gulf continues to separate the richest people, mostly whites, from the poor, which includes the great majority of blacks, people of mixed race, and Indians.

The various ethnic groups found in Brazil

46

WHICH IS BRAZIL'S MOST BEAUTIFUL CITY?

Famed for its bay, its Sugar Loaf rock, and its beaches with enchanting names like Copacabana, Rio de Janeiro is the "cidade maravilhosa," the marvelous city.

Between mountainous peaks and the seashore, Rio de Janeiro is set amid the loveliest scenery a city could ever have. In Portuguese, its name means "January River," as a reminder of the landing on this paradisiac site in January 1502 by sailors of King Manuel I of Portugal.

The capital of Brazil until 1960, when Brasilia was built to bring people and trade to the interior region, Rio and its surroundings form a metropolis of over five million inhabitants that has long lived on the myth of easy living. The highly charged atmosphere of this city has always attracted personalities as flamboyant as the nocturnal festivities in which they take part. The inhabitants of Rio—the Cariocas—display a mixture of striking contrasts in which exist, side by side, the greatest wealth and extreme poverty, violence and a relaxed attitude, exuberance and human drama, the golden rule being, "Never do today what you can put off until tomorrow."

Attracted by this **megalopolis**, thousands of Brazilians from the countryside flock to the shantytowns—called favelas—encircling it, in search of a better future. Under the unchanging gaze of the statue of Christ the Redeemer on Mount Corcovado is played out the painful survival of countless children, who day after day, defying the "**death squads**," search for something to eat and somewhere to live.

Left: Christ of the Andes between Chile and Argentina
Right: The Copacabana beach

WHERE DOES THE BIGGEST CARNIVAL TAKE PLACE?

Though the carnivals in Latin America and the Caribbean countries vie with each other in splendor, there is still one that outdoes them all: the Carnival of Rio de Janeiro.

In Brazil, carnival festivities are held in various places, such as Salvador de Bahia, birthplace of the **samba**, and Recife in the Northeast where it is still traditional. But the most famous one is unquestionably the one in Rio. Every year, during the week before Lent, the city goes into a trance. For months ahead of time, the Cariocas have been preparing for it and saving up the money needed to make the most beautiful costumes that will be exhibited on the most beautiful floats. For months ahead of time, the samba schools have vied in imagination and musical creativity to be stars in the festival's sky for the few days of delirium and dreams. But the sadness of the aftermath of Carnival is as intensely felt as the joyousness that preceded it.

This festival is a typically Brazilian way of drowning in music an alarmingly commonplace quality of life, made up for many people of violence and insecurity. But the Carnival is also an example of the diversity of the Brazilian population, with its emphasis on its African and European heritages.

Carnival in Rio de Janeiro

IS THERE A CITY OF THE FUTURE IN BRAZIL?

When President Kubitschek was elected in 1955, he vowed that he would give his country a futuristic capital, built in the heart of vast virgin land: Brasilia.

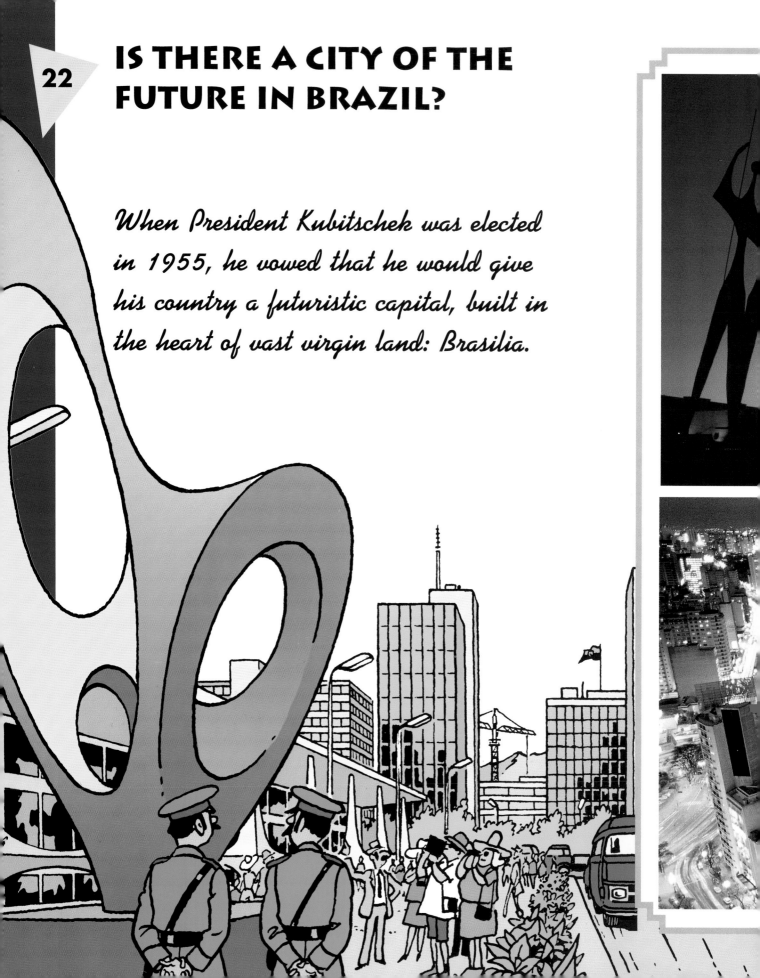

The superb official buildings of Brasilia, designed by the architect **Oscar Niemeyer**, are the pride of the whole country. City planner Lucio Costa designed Brasilia in the shape of an airplane: the residential and commercial areas are the wings, the government buildings have the pilot's position, with the executive, judicial, and legislative buildings at the nose, and hotels, a sports arena, and fairgrounds heading toward the tail. But despite careful planning of the city, contradictions have appeared. The disparity of wealth has led to the shanty-towns that surround this "ideal city" with pockets of poverty.

Huge São Paulo, the New York of South America, is the principal business city of Brazil and its industrial heart. The seriousness and the hardworking attitude of its inhabitants are as well known as the relaxed attitude of the Cariocas, the residents of Rio.

As for Salvador de Bahia, on the northeast coast, it seems to be a little sister-city of Rio's: Here too, in a superb natural setting, the Bahianos' relaxed attitude and sense of fun are expressed to the full. But Bahia still remains primarily the heart of Brazil's culture, marked by a blend of African sensitivity and Portuguese lifestyle, in culinary art, music, and dance.

Top: Brasilia
Bottom: São Paulo

WHAT IS THE BRAZILIANS' FAVORITE SPORT?

Soccer is a typically Brazilian passion. Brazil has provided the sport with some of the best players in the world.

Brazilians experience soccer with the same exuberance that characterizes everything they do. The Cariocas' hero-worship of the soccer gods is equal to the stadium where they are seen. At the Maracana field in Rio, where over 200,000 people are crammed in, the famous "King" **Pelé** glorified a sport that has become, through the magic of the game and the ambiance in the bleachers, an amazing show. In fact, Brazil is now the only four-time winner of the World Cup.

Bands and sambas rhythmically match the wild career of the ball, watched by a colorful audience that with one hand waves flags and kites, and with the other keeps a transistor radio glued to one ear. Drums, fire-crackers, shouts, and jeers mark the progress of the *futebol* match. But far beyond the biggest stadium in the world, the whole town is bubbling, frantically following the movements of the players.

Once more, Rio will not sleep until after a wild night's talk over a *feijoada*, the national dish, a thick soup based on black beans garnished with pieces of beef or pork. The Cariocas eat it with the same gusto that matches their funny and ironic comments during the eventful night.

Top: Maracana Stadium in Rio de Janeiro
Bottom: The Cariocas

WHERE ARE THE IGUAÇU FALLS?

Located on the Paraná River, flowing through Brazil, Paraguay, and Argentina, the Iguaçu Falls are the most spectacular in the world: about 237 feet (72 m) high, and over 2 miles (3.2 km) across.

The Iguaçu River is a tributary of the Paraná. Rising in the heart of Brazil, the Paraná forms a huge loop before emptying into the Atlantic. Its estuary is called Rio de la Plata, the "silver river." Iguaçu is an Indian word meaning "great waters."

On its way, the Paraná has collected the Paraguay, which drains the huge Pantanal swamp, eight times the size of Maryland, a veritable paradise for 600 species of birds and many other aquatic animals. This river, much longer than many streams that empty into the sea, also gives its name to an isolated, archaic, little tropical state. The Guarani Indians, once protected by the Jesuits in their missions, still make up the bulk of the population. With no resources except cattle raising on the desert plateaus of the Gran Chaco, deprived of access to the sea, and ruined by successive dictators, Paraguay is the poorest country in Latin America.

On the other side of Brazil, in Venezuela, is the Salto Angel, or Angel Falls, a waterfall 3,212 feet (979 m) high, the highest in the world. The name it bears is not an allusion to the acrobats' "angel's leap," but in memory of the American pilot and gold prospector Jimmy Angel, who discovered it in 1935, in an area that is still very wild today. Salto Angel is located on the course of the Caroni, a tributary of the Orinoco, which, although it is the Amazon's little Venezuelan brother, is 1,284 miles (2,066 km) long anyway!

Top: Iguaçu Falls
Bottom: Salto Angel

WHAT DOES THE NAME "VENEZUELA" MEAN?

In 1499, observing the houses built on stilts and the canoes of the Indians in this region of America, Vespucci dubbed it "Little Venice."

Top: A village built on pilings in Venezuela
Bottom left: Oil wells in Maracaibo
Bottom right: Venezuela children

Rich in natural resources (there are abundant mineral resources in the Orinoco basin) but unable to make the investments needed to work them, Venezuela was for many years one of the poorest countries in South America. At the beginning of the twentieth century, European fleets even went so far as to blockade Venezuelan ports, calling for repayment of loans!

The development in 1917 of an immense oilfield located under the Maracaibo Basin changed the country's destiny almost overnight. It was the first time oil was extracted by drilling under water from derricks set up on crude wooden platforms, forerunners of modern oceanic offshore plat-forms. Venezuela soon became the richest country in the region, thereby deserving its name, borrowed from the most opulent city in Italy. It wasn't until after 1958, however, that this extraordinary source of wealth, initially grabbed by a handful of businessmen protected by successive dictators, was finally of some benefit to the population.

Since then, Venezuela has become a democracy, despite the still enormous burden of national debt that from time to time gives rise to protests or even revolt (as in 1989) on the part of a population that has remained poor. Far away from the luxury and huge green areas of the capital, Caracas, the Venezuelan peasant is hardly any better off than his Brazilian or Colombian neighbors.

26

WHICH IS THE LARGEST CITY IN THE AMERICAS?

Bigger than the cities of New York or Los Angeles, here is Mexico City, the "megalopolis," with 15.3 million inhabitants, or almost!

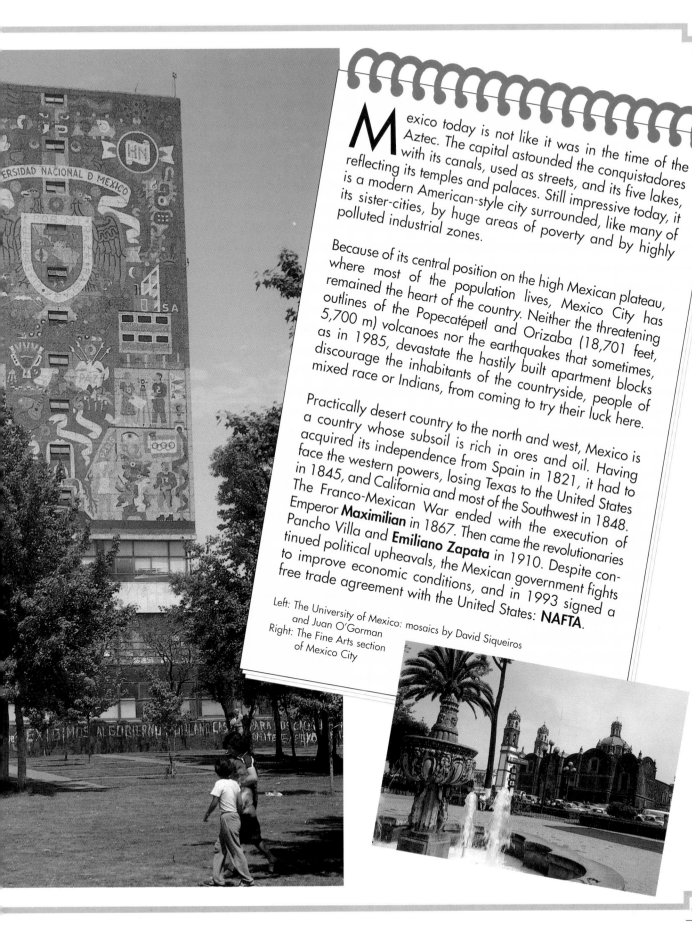

Mexico today is not like it was in the time of the Aztec. The capital astounded the conquistadores with its canals, used as streets, and its five lakes, reflecting its temples and palaces. Still impressive today, it is a modern American-style city surrounded, like many of its sister-cities, by huge areas of poverty and by highly polluted industrial zones.

Because of its central position on the high Mexican plateau, where most of the population lives, Mexico City has remained the heart of the country. Neither the threatening outlines of the Popecatépetl and Orizaba (18,701 feet, 5,700 m) volcanoes nor the earthquakes that sometimes, as in 1985, devastate the hastily built apartment blocks discourage the inhabitants of the countryside, people of mixed race or Indians, from coming to try their luck here.

Practically desert country to the north and west, Mexico is a country whose subsoil is rich in ores and oil. Having acquired its independence from Spain in 1821, it had to face the western powers, losing Texas to the United States in 1845, and California and most of the Southwest in 1848. The Franco-Mexican War ended with the execution of Emperor **Maximilian** in 1867. Then came the revolutionaries Pancho Villa and **Emiliano Zapata** in 1910. Despite continued political upheavals, the Mexican government fights to improve economic conditions, and in 1993 signed a free trade agreement with the United States: **NAFTA**.

Left: The University of Mexico: mosaics by David Siqueiros and Juan O'Gorman
Right: The Fine Arts section of Mexico City

WHERE DID THE CARIBS LIVE?

The Caribs, the first Indians to greet Christopher Columbus in America, disappeared from the Antilles in less than 200 years, decimated by disease and forced labor.

Only their name remains, attributed to the sea that washes the islands where the Carib Indians once lived. The present inhabitants of the Antilles are descendants of the European colonists and African slaves who worked in the vast plantations of sugarcane, tobacco, and tropical fruits.

Though the Windward Islands are still French administrative districts (such as Guadelupe and Martinique), the three islands of the Greater Antilles finally acquired their independence. With few natural resources, their fates are all very different. Indeed, Cuba, a Communist enclave, has long been led, since 1959, by the iron hand of **Fidel Castro**, while in Haiti, the military junta that succeeded the oppressive Duvalier regime had ousted President Aristide, the first democratically chosen leader. The U.S. government succeeded in having Aristide reinstated October 15, 1994.

Neither poverty nor tropical hurricanes nor terrible volcanic eruptions seem to be able to take away from the inhabitants of these sunny islands their taste for festivals and multicolored costumes, their lilting speech, and their heartwarming music. The Antilles attract many tourists from the United States and Europe, particularly in the winter.

A beach in the Caribbean
Foreground: Young twins in the Antilles

28

WHO WERE THE FILIBUSTERS?

On the route of the Spanish galleons bringing home gold from the New World, the Caribbean Sea became a paradise for pirates. They were the filibusters...

The name comes from an old Dutch word meaning lawless freebooters, or plunderers. They were also known as buccaneers , because they had adopted the native habit of smoking the meat of the cattle they hunted in the islands on a grill called a *boucan*. Adventurers on the seas, the **filibusters** founded, in particular on the island of Tortuga, off the coast of Haiti, veritable republics of ruffians whose skull and crossbones flag spread terror among the Spanish captains.

The most famous of them were Henry Morgan, Blackbeard, Captain Kidd, and Jean Laffite, who in 1812, defended the French colony in Louisiana from the British. Sometimes the European countries allied themselves with these freelancers of the sea. Then, having become **privateers**, they had documents authorizing them to pillage enemy vessels!

The ships that cross these waters today on their way to the Panama Canal are no longer afraid of pirates, but rather of hurricanes and shoals. These have caused so many shipwrecks and mysterious disappearances that the **"Bermuda Triangle"** legend has arisen. But the legend, which persists, does not stop the many luxury liners with their thousands of tourists, as well as sport-fishermen, and divers seeking sunken treasure from visiting the area.

Left: A port in the Caribbean
Top right: The cannon at Port-Royal in Jamaica

29

WHAT HAS BECOME OF THE BLACKS IN LATIN AMERICA?

From peaceful coexistence with whites in Brazil, to the violent confrontations that have marked the history of Haiti, the fate of millions of Latin-American blacks has been very varied.

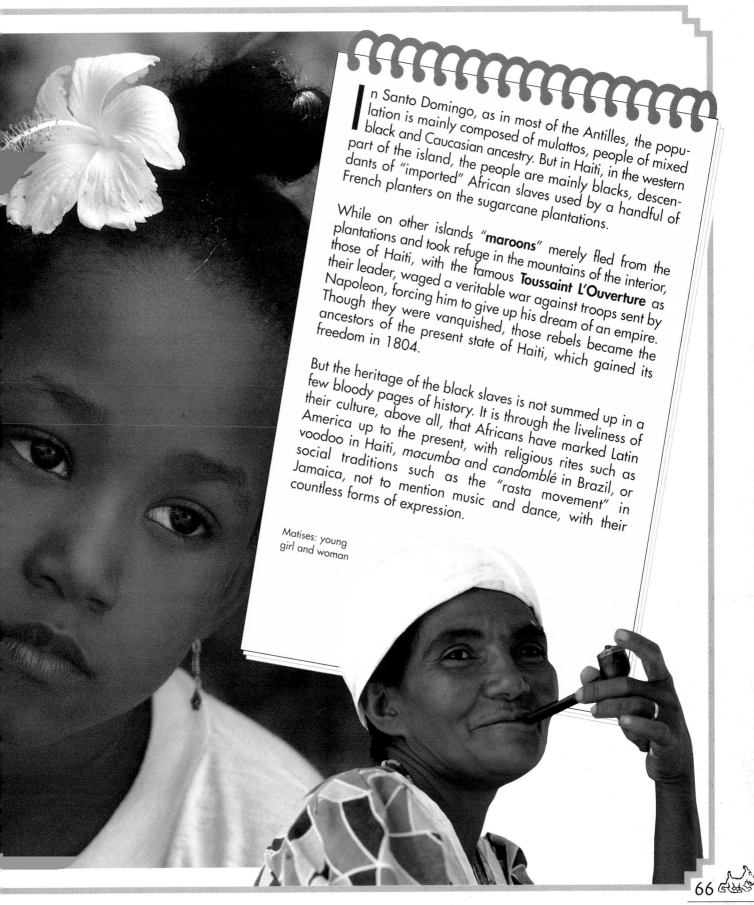

In Santo Domingo, as in most of the Antilles, the population is mainly composed of mulattos, people of mixed black and Caucasian ancestry. But in Haiti, in the western part of the island, the people are mainly blacks, descendants of "imported" African slaves used by a handful of French planters on the sugarcane plantations.

While on other islands "**maroons**" merely fled from the plantations and took refuge in the mountains of the interior, those of Haiti, with the famous **Toussaint L'Ouverture** as their leader, waged a veritable war against troops sent by Napoleon, forcing him to give up his dream of an empire. Though they were vanquished, those rebels became the ancestors of the present state of Haiti, which gained its freedom in 1804.

But the heritage of the black slaves is not summed up in a few bloody pages of history. It is through the liveliness of their culture, above all, that Africans have marked Latin America up to the present, with religious rites such as voodoo in Haiti, macumba and candomblé in Brazil, or social traditions such as the "rasta movement" in Jamaica, not to mention music and dance, with their countless forms of expression.

Matises: young
girl and woman

30

WHERE DOES "REGGAE" COME FROM?

This rhythmic music started in Jamaica, and became world famous in the 1970s when the singer Bob Marley adapted it to rock.

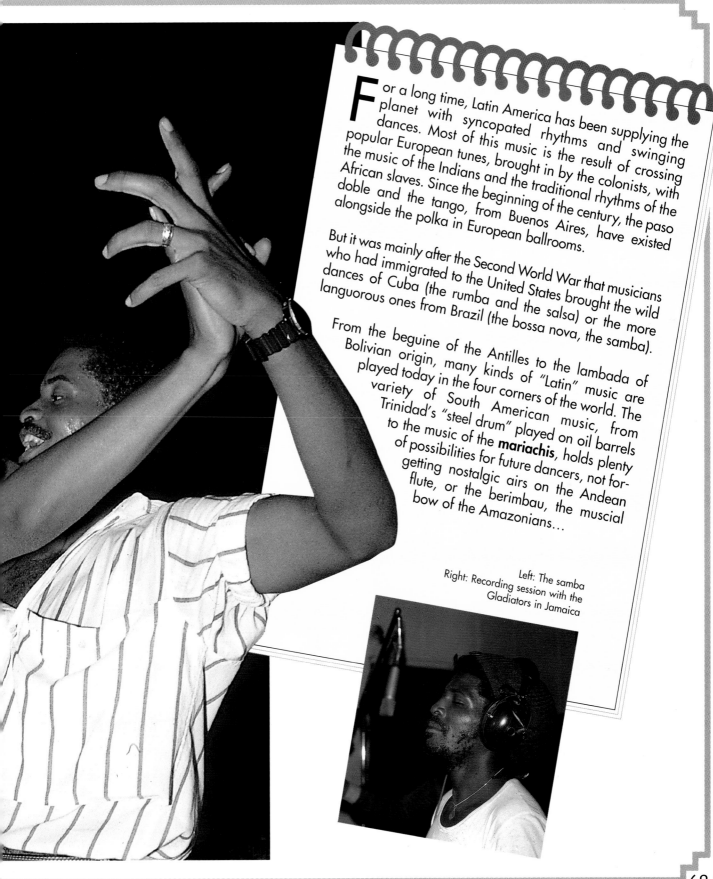

For a long time, Latin America has been supplying the planet with syncopated rhythms and swinging dances. Most of this music is the result of crossing popular European tunes, brought in by the colonists, with the music of the Indians and the traditional rhythms of the African slaves. Since the beginning of the century, the paso doble and the tango, from Buenos Aires, have existed alongside the polka in European ballrooms.

But it was mainly after the Second World War that musicians who had immigrated to the United States brought the wild dances of Cuba (the rumba and the salsa) or the more languorous ones from Brazil (the bossa nova, the samba).

From the beguine of the Antilles to the lambada of Bolivian origin, many kinds of "Latin" music are played today in the four corners of the world. The variety of South American music, from Trinidad's "steel drum" played on oil barrels to the music of the **mariachis**, holds plenty of possibilities for future dancers, not forgetting nostalgic airs on the Andean flute, or the berimbau, the muscial bow of the Amazonians…

Left: The samba
Right: Recording session with the
Gladiators in Jamaica

A

AMAZON : South American river that rises in Peru and empties into the Atlantic. It is the world's largest in terms of the area of its basin, and second to the Nile for length (4,000 miles, 6,400 km). If like most geographers we consider the Apurimac as its mother stream, the length would be about 4,390 miles (7,025 km).

AZTEC : Indians who came from the north, the Aztec entered the present valley of Mexico City in the thirteenth century and founded their principal city, Tenochtitlán (the future Mexico City), in 1325. At the beginning of the fifteenth century, the Aztec Empire extended over the whole of central Mexico, but when faced with the Spanish conquistadores, Emperor Montezuma was unable to stand up to them. The empire was dismantled around 1525, and the last emperor, Cuauhtémoc, was hanged.

B

BANDEIRANTES : Portuguese adventurers who arrived in Brazil in 1600 seeking gold and slaves.

BERMUDA TRIANGLE : an area, located in the Atlantic Ocean among Puerto Rico, the Bermudas, and the Bahamas, in which many ships and aircraft have disappeared without trace. Hurricanes, poor oceanic maps, unknown and often violent currents, and uncharted shoals have led to many shipwrecks. The Gulf Stream, fast and turbulent, is capable of erasing all signs of shipwreck, however, leading to a sense of mystery and legend about the area.

C

CACIQUE : native chieftain of certain tribes in the Americas.

CANDOMBLÉ : a rite of African origin performed in the state of Bahia. Ordination of the priests takes place through the ceremony of headshaving, ritual bathing, and applying feathers and chicken or goat blood to the forehead. The ceremony is accompanied by muffled drumbeats, African chants, and frenzied dances intended to put the initiates into a state of trance.

CAOUTCHOUC (PERUVIAN WORD) : rubber; impermeable elastic substance derived from the latex of various tropical trees (ficus, hevea, and others), or artificially manufactured.

CAYMAN (CARIBBEAN WORD) : alligatorlike reptile of Central and South America, 16 to 20 feet (5 to 6 m) long.

D

DEATH SQUADS : groups of right-wing hit men employed by the government who practice, in most large cities in Brazil, the summary liquidation without trial of people who have "fallen into disgrace according to the opinion of the police." Victims are almost always from the most underprivileged groups of the population: inhabitants of the *favelas*. A large number of those executed are youths under 20, almost all blacks, or people of mixed race. The killers work under unclear alliances with the military police and private interests of the rich ruling class.

DEFORESTATION : destruction of forests.

DUVALIER FAMILY : Dr. Francis Duvalier ruled Haiti as an absolute dictator from 1957 until his death in 1971. His son Jean Claude (Baby Doc) Duvalier ruled until 1986, when he was forced to flee the country.

E

EMILIANO ZAPATA : Indian revolutionary leader of Mexico in 1910 who supported agrarian reforms for his people.

F

FAVELAS : groups of dwellings without plumbing or power; shantytowns located outside the large cities of Brazil.

FAZENDA : large estate in Brazil.

FIDEL CASTRO (SANTIAGO DE CUBA, 1927) : Cuban revolutionary and statesman. In 1956 he landed in Cuba with some supporters, organized guerillas against the dictator, Batista, and took power after the latter's fall in 1959.

FILIBUSTERS : pirates who, in the seventeenth and eighteenth centuries, roamed the Antilles coasts and laid waste the Spanish possessions.

FITZCARRALDO : name given to Brian Fitzgerald, rubber baron, whose arrogant folly was dramatized in a film by Werner Herzog.

FRANCISCO DE ORELLANA (1511–1546) : Spanish explorer in the sixteenth century. Pizarro's companion at the conquest of Peru, he explored regions east of the Andean Mountains, then reached the Amazon, down which he navigated to the Atlantic.

I

INFLATABLE TIRE : first designed in 1845 by the Scot Robert William Thomson. It began to advance with John Boyd Dunlop in 1888 and the Michelin brothers in 1891.

J

JESUITS : Roman Catholics who, in the seventeenth century, built missions around which Indian villages were set up. Their objective was to protect the Guarani tribes from slave dealers. The Jesuits thus controlled the region for over a century, supervising the building of Indian cities that sometimes reached 5,000 inhabitants. In 1756 the missions were attacked and overthrown by supporters of slavery; the Jesuits were expelled and most of the Indians exterminated.

JUNTA : administrative, political, or military assembly in Spain, Portugal, or Latin America; name given to governments that resulted from military coups d'état.

M

MANIOC : shrub found in tropical regions, the root of which provides an edible starch, tapioca.

MARIACHIS : in Mexico, strolling musicians dressed in colorful costume who perform on the street, in restaurants, and at parties.

MAROON : in colonial America, referred to a runaway slave.

MAXIMILIAN : brother of Emperor Franz-Josef, archduke of Austria. In 1863, Napoleon offered him the imperial crown of Mexico. Captured by Benito Juárez, the revolutionary leader of Mexico, president from 1858 to 1872, Maximilian was executed by rifle fire in 1867.

MAYA : Indian people of Central America whose brilliant civilization extended over nearly all the present territory of Guatemala, Honduras, and southern Mexico. Mayan society, which was warlike and mercantile, had a strong hierarchical structure. It was dominated by an aristocracy that controlled slaves and prisoners who did the heaviest work. Today there remain only 330,000 Maya, scattered in Guatemala and Mexico.

MEGALOPOLIS : very large urban center.

MINAS GERAIS : state of Brazil. A little larger than France, it has a population of about 15 million. Minas Gerais means "general mines." Abundant seams have supplied the whole world with gold, diamonds, and iron ore.

N

NAFTA : North American Free Trade Agreement between the United States, Mexico, and Canada to create a trade zone similar to that of the European Common Market.

O

OLMEC : ancient people of Mexico from about 2000 to 200 B.C. Traces of Olmec influence have been found in all the peoples of Mexico. The invention of the Meso-American calendar, perfected by the Maya, has been attributed to the Olmec.

OSCAR SOARES NIEMEYER : architect born in Rio de Janeiro in 1907. After completing numerous construction projects, he was charged by President Kubitschek with the architecture of the government buildings in the new capital, Brasilia. Neimeyer was also one of the architects responsible for designing the United Nations headquarters in New York City.

P

PANCHO VILLA (1878–1923) : Mexican revolutionary general. A perpetual rebel, going from one cause to another, he turned himself in to the legal government in 1920 and was assassinated three years later.

PELÉ (EDSON ARANTES DO NASCIMENTO) : known as "King Pelé," this Brazilian soccer player was discovered when Brazil won the World Cup in 1958. Pelé compelled recognition as the world's best player. A remarkable goal scorer, he also showed excellent leadership.

PERÓN (JUAN DOMINGO) (1895–1974) : Argentinian politician who was elected president of the republic in 1946 and established the so-called "spirit of fairness" that won the support of the clergy, the army, the leftist parties, and the extreme right-wing nationalists. The doctrine, which was very popular in the beginning but became a dictatorship in 1950, combined social measures, anti-American policies, Catholicism, repression, and nationalization. Perón was overturned by a putsch in 1955 and fled to Spain.

S

SAMBA : popular Brazilian dance of African origin, in double time with a syncopated rhythm.

SELVA : means "rain forest" in Portuguese.

SHAMAN : magician priest who practices divination and medical care by communing with the spirits of nature during a mystical journey of trance and ecstasy.

T

TAPIR : hoofed herbivorous mammal that can grow to over 6 feet (2 m), it has short legs and a snout that extends into a short trunk.

TOLTEC : Indian people who settled in the north of present-day Mexico City between about 900 and 1200 A.D. Several of their pyramids contain the image of Quetzalcoatl, a Toltec ruler the Indians came to look on as a god. The Toltec are believed to have influenced the Maya.

TOUCAN : climbing bird with brightly colored plumage and a huge beak; lives in the tropical forests of South America.

TOUSSAINT L'OUVERTURE (1743–1803) : Former slave who became a Haitian politician and ruler of Haiti. He called upon blacks to support the French government, which had just abolished slavery (1794). He stated his intention of creating a black republic, and defended the island against the British and the Spanish. When Napoleon announced the reestablishment of slavery (1802), Toussaint resisted. He was arrested, taken to France, and imprisoned in the fort at Joux, where he died shortly before Haiti became independent.

V

VOODOO : cult imported into the Antilles by black slaves.

Y

YANOMAMIS : Indians of South America. They occupy border areas between Brazil and Venezuela and lead a semi-nomadic life. Once 22,000 strong, with 9,000 in Brazil in 1987, they were the largest Indian group to have been untouched by outside civilizations. Their territories have since been invaded by gold prospectors, and they have been victims of massacres, diseases outside their race, rapes, and deportation.

B.C.
3000

Start of the Bronze Age in Nile and
Tigris-Euphrates river valleys

Valdivia culture in Ecuador: semi-settled
populations

2000

Hammurabi establishes the
Babylonian Empire (c. 1800)

Cultivation of manioc in the Amazon
Region and Orinoco

1000

Metal coins used in China and Lydia (800)

Olmec civilization in Mexico
Start of a calendar system and writing in
Central America

0

Chinese make paper (c. 100)
Fall of Rome (476)

Oldest Mayan stone monument (dated 292)
in Tikal

500

Muslims defeated near Tours (732), stopping
the spread of Islam into Western Europe

End of the classical Mayan period in Mexico
(c. 900)

1000

Marco Polo's travels in China (1271–1295)

Christopher Columbus lands at Guanahani
(San Salvador) (1492)
The Treaty of Tordesillas (1494)

1500

Sir Francis Drake begins trip around the
world (1577)

Pedro Alvares Cabral lands in Brazil (1500)
Conquest of Mexico by Cortez (1519–1526)
Orellana reaches the Amazon delta (1542)

1600

Jamestown, the first permanent settlement in
North America, is founded (1609)

Captain Pedro de Texeira navigates up the
Amazon from Belem to Quito (1637–1638)

1700

The adoption of the U.S. Constitution (1789)
George Washington inaugurated as first
president of the United States (1789)

Publication in Paris of Father Fritz's map of
the course of the Amazon (1717)
Humboldt and Bonpland's journey from the
Orinoco to the Rio Negro (1799–1800)

1800

Construction of Stephenson's locomotive (1814)
Monroe Doctrine issued (1823)

Independence of Brazil (1822)
Lifetime of Pancho Villa (1878–1923)

1900
A.D.

The U.S. announces the Alliance for Progress
(1961)

Founding of FUNAI (National Foundation
for Indians) (1972)
The Brazilian Constitution recognizes Indian
land rights (1988)

MEXICO
• **Mexico City**
▲ *Popocatépetl*
▲ *Orizaba*   *Yucatán*
MEXICO
BELIZE
GUATEMALA
EL SALVADOR   HONDURAS
NICARAGUA

CUBA
JAMAICA
HAITI
DOMINICAN
REPUBLIC
**Santo
Domingo**
PUERTO RICO

CARIBBEAN SEA

*The Azores***

ATLANTIC
OCEAN

Guadeloupe
Dominica
Martinique
Santa Lucia
Barbados
Grenada
*Trinidad
and
Tobago*

COSTA RICA
PANAMA
*Panama
Canal*
• **Panama City**

Maracaibo • **Caracas**
Orinoco Plain
Caroní
VENEZUELA
COLOMBIA

SURINAME
GUYANA
FRENCH
GUIANA

*Galapagos
Islands*

ECUADOR
• **Quito**
PERU

Japurá   *Rio Negro*
Amazon
Manaus •
Amazon Region

Belém

Urubamba
Apurímac
A N D E S   M O U N T A I N S

BOLIVIA

• **Rondônia**

*Mato Grosso
Plateau*

BRAZIL

São Fransisco

Brasília •

Salvador •

MINAS GERAIS   *Ouro Preto*

PARAGUAY
Asuncion •

*Iguaçu
Falls*

**Rio de
Janeiro**

PACIFIC
OCEAN

CHILE

ARGENTINA

Uruguay
URUGUAY

Santiago •

Rio Colorado

Rio Negro

• **Buenos Aires**

ATLANTIC
OCEAN

*Tierra
del
Fuego*

*Falkland
Islands*

*Cape
Horn*

0   1000   2000   3000 km

*Located 800 miles (1300 km) west of Portugal. Claimed for Portugal in 1431 by Gonzalo Cabral.

index

bibliography

THE AMAZON REGION, FOR READERS FROM 7 TO 77

Abbott, Elizabeth.
Haiti: The Duvaliers and Their Legacy.
New York: McGraw-Hill, 1988.

Bender, Evelyn.
Brazil.
New York: Chelsea House, 1990.

Chagnon, Napoleon.
Yanomano: The Last Days of Eden.
New York: Harcourt Brace Jovanovich, 1992.

Cousteau, Jacques.
Jacques Cousteau's Amazon Journey.
New York: Harry N. Abrams, 1984.

Hemming, John.
Amazon Frontier: The Defeat of the Brazilian Indians.
Cambridge: Harvard University Press, 1987.

Henley, Paul.
Amazon Indians.
Morristown, New York: Silver Burdett, 1980.

Lizot, Jacques.
Tales of the Yanomani.
Cambridge: Harvard University Press, 1985.

Lye, Keith.
Argentina.
London: Franklin Watts, 1986.

Morrison, Marion.
The Amazon Rain Forest and Its People.
New York: Thomson Learning, 1993.

Morrison, Marion.
Venezuela.
New York: Chelsea House, 1987.

Reynolds, Jan.
Amazon Basin: Vanishing Cultures.
San Diego: Harcourt Brace & Co., 1993.

Siy, Alexandra.
The Brazilian Rain Forest.
New York: Dillon Press, 1992.

Smith, Anthony.
Explorers of the Amazon.
New York: Viking Press, 1990.

Waterlow, Julia.
Brazil.
New York: Bookwright Press, 1992.

PHOTO CREDITS

All the photographs were taken by L. Girard, except the following:

—Cover, p. 15 (bottom), p. 17 (lower right), p. 19 (lower right), p. 21 (lower left), p. 25, p. 27 (bottom), p. 29 (top), p. 31 (upper left and lower right), p. 35 (top), p. 55 (top): G. Civet

—p. 11, p. 13 (lower left), p. 19 (left), p. 21 (upper left), p. 23, p. 27 (top), p. 29 (bottom), p. 31 (lower right), p. 43, p. 45 (lower right), p. 59 (lower right): A-S. Tiberghien

—p. 15 (top), p. 17 (left), p. 41 (bottom): J. Cornet

—p. 29 (bottom) M. D. Sutton/Superstock

—p. 33, p. 61 (lower right), p. 65 (lower right), p. 69 (lower right): F. Guerlain

—p. 41 (top) National Library, Paris. Casterman Archives

—p. 57 (bottom), p. 59 (upper and lower left), p. 61 (left): M. Aubert